Johannes Hösle

Whatever Befalls

Poems from
Dietenbronn Neurological Clinic

Translated by Marc Estrin

Fomite
Burlington, VT

Poems: Johannes Hösle
Translation: Marc Estrin
Cover image: *Langsam auf dem Weg*, a print from the series, *Terra Incognita*, by
Gisela Conrad, graphic artist, who lived and worked in Regensburg, Germany
ISBN-13: 978-1-953236-73-9
Library of Congress Control Number: 2022935992

Fomite
58 Peru Street
Burlington, VT 05401
www.fomitepress.com
05/31/2022

Acknowledgements

The translator wishes to thank the poet's daughter, Adriana Hösle Borra, first for her gift of these poems in her husband Antonello Borra's beautiful German-Italian version, and even more, for her help with this translation in general, and regarding particular aspects of her father's writing and Dietenbronn experience.

Inhaltsverzeichnis/Contents

Vorwort	2
Preface	4
Der Waldbrand	6
The Forest Fire	7
Das Bett	8
The Bed	9
Die Ameisen	10
The Ants	11
Die Stundung	12
Deferring Payment	13
Die Diagnose	14
The Diagnosis	16
Miquel Martí i Pol	18
Miquel Martí i Pol	19
Die Gleichgültigkeit	20
Indifference	21
Heinz-Peter	22
Heinz-Peter	24
Nacht	26
Night	27
Andreas	28
Andreas	29
Der Aufzug	30
The Lift	31
Der Tümpel	32
The Pond	33
Die Evers-Diät	34
The Evers Diet	35
Im oberen Rottal	36

In the Upper Rot Valley 37
Mit Blütenzweigen im Arm 38
With Flowering Branches in her Arms 39
Die Telefonistin 40
Someone on the Phone 42
Die Hand 44
Hand 45
Die Coppelius-Puppe 46
The Coppelius Doll 47
Die Pony-Ranch 48
The Pony Ranch 50
Die Wanderung 52
Hike 53
Das Geländer 54
The Railing 55
Die Birke 56
The Birch Tree 57
Stuten und Töchter 58
Horses and Daughters 59
Der alte Mann 60
The Old Man 62
Women's Lib 64
Women's Lib 65
Pfingsten 66
Pentecost 68
Tat twam asi 70
Tat twam asi 71
Die Heimkehr 72
Going Home 73

Wir müssen von ganzem Herzen alles, was uns trifft, willkommen heißen, wir dürfen auch innerlich nicht murren, ja uns nicht einmal wundern.

Marc Aurel

Accept heartily whatever befalls you and don't grumble or even be surprised about it.

Marcus Aurelius

Vorwort

Daß diese Texte mindestens typographisch als
Gedichte angeordnet sind, geht darauf zurück,
daß wegen einer Lähmung meine Handschrift
bis auf weiteres nicht leserlich war. Dazu kam
eine Sehstörung. So war vorübergehend jede auf
Lesen und Schreiben beruhende intellektuelle
Tätigkeit unmöglich. Ich war meinen Sorgen
ausgeliefert und den Eindrücken der Klinik. Nur
wenn ich sie fixierte, konnte ich verhindern, daß
sie zu Obsessionen wurden. Es war mir daher
eine große Erleichterung, als die Schrift langsam
wieder leserlich wurde, und der Schlagschatten
aus meiner Optik verschwand. Daß ich Gedichte
schrieb, hatte zunächst einen praktischen
Grund. Es galt in meinem Gedächtnis möglichst
konzise und komprimierte Texte zu speichern.
Dazu kamen therapeutische Überlegungen:
Rhythmen haben etwas Beschwörendes,
machen das Chaos von diagnostischem Schock
und durcheinanderwirbelnden Impressionen
überschaubarer, dichten lecke Stellen ab
und gestatten auch noch ein Minimum an
Persönlichkeitsentfaltung, wo sie eine von außen
kommende Organisation wie im Gefängnis und
in der Kaserne nur mit hundert Einschränkungen
möglich macht.

Der größte Widerspruch einer Klinikerfahrung ist, daß man auf sich zurückgeworfen wird und dabei seine Haut verliert. In meinem besonderen Fall fiel der Krankenhausaufenthalt in meine nähere Heimat. Das muß erwähnt werden, um die wiederholten Hinweise auf Früheres zu erklären. Ich hätte mir diese subjektive Komponente nicht erlaubt, wenn sie nicht entscheidend mein psychisches Befinden bestimmt hätten. Wahrscheinlich bringt diese Verknüpfung von Anfang und Ende allen wilden Protest zur Ruhe. Das kann auch erklären, warum diese Gedichte manchmal so konservativ wirken.

Aber die Kategorien reaktionär/revolutionär spielen im Krankenhaus kaum eine Rolle. Hier gilt ein anderes Koordinatensystem. Es gibt Kranke, die Besserung verspüren, und solche, die keine Hoffnung mehr haben. Das kann soweit gehen, daß sie – obwohl sie noch sprechen können – darauf verzichten, einen Gruß zu erwidern oder sich an einem Gespräch zu beteiligen. Diese Kranken stellen keine Fragen mehr, sind scheinbar an keiner Antwort mehr interessiert.

Bei allen Vorbehalten sind diese Texte ein geschlossener Zyklus. Die Zahl der Gedichte entspricht den in der Klinik verbrachten Tagen. Es galt auszuwählen wie bei der Zusammenstellung eines Albums. Als solches präsentiert es sich nun dem Leser.

Preface

That these texts are at least typographically arranged as poems is due to the fact that my handwriting was illegible for the time being because of a paralysis. There were also visual problems. So any intellectual activity based on reading and writing was temporarily impossible. I was at the mercy of my worries and my impressions of the clinic. Only by staring them in the face could I keep them from becoming obsessions. It was therefore a great relief to me when my writing slowly became legible again and the shadows disappeared from my vision. My first reason for writing poetry was practical. It was important to save texts as concise and compressed as possible in my memory. In addition, there were therapeutic considerations: Rhythms have something evocative, make the chaos of diagnostic shock and contrasting impressions easier to grasp, seal up leaks and also allow a bit of personality development, while an outside organization such as a prison or barracks, makes that possible only with a hundred restrictions.

The greatest contradiction in the clinical experience is that you are thrown back on yourself and become more vulnerable in the process. In my particular case, my hospitalization happened to be very close to where I was born. I mention this to explain my repeated references to the past. I would not have allowed myself this subjective component if it had not decisively helped my psychological well-being. A link between the beginning and the end probably calms all wild protests. It can also explain why these poems sometimes seem so conservative.

But the categories reactionary/revolutionary play hardly any role in the hospital. A different coordinate system applies here. There are sick people who feel better, and others who have no more hope. They may be at a point which – although they can still speak – they never return a greeting or take part in a conversation. Such patients no longer ask questions and are apparently no longer interested in answers.

All this being said, these texts are a finished cycle. The number of poems corresponds to the number of days spent in the clinic. I had to pick and choose, as when putting together an album. As such, it now presents itself to the reader.

Der Waldbrand

Die Krankheit
breitet sich aus
wie Waldbrand.
Plötzlich stieben
die Schmerzen
als Funken
an eine Stelle,
die sicher schien.
Woher kommt
die pelzige Hand
und das Kribbelgelenk,
wenn die Schulter
und der obere Arm
vorerst noch gar nicht betroffen?
Oder die Doppeloptik,
die dich tagelang narrt?
Ist die akute Phase beendigt,
zählst du
das noch Vorhandene
nach einem Brand.

The Forest Fire

Disease
spreads
like a forest fire.
It suddenly pushes
a spark
of pain
into someplace
that seemed safe.
Where does that tingling hand
come from
and the buzzing joint,
if the shoulder
and the upper arm
are not at all affected yet?
Or the double vision,
that fools you for days?
When the acute phase is over,
you count
what's left
after the fire.

Das Bett

Der Name der Krankheit trägt dich hinweg
wie eine Welle bei hohem Seegang.
Die Konsequenzen werden vorerst nicht abgewogen.
Die Panik dröhnt wie Wasser in beiden Ohren.

Aber da ist die Müdigkeit,
aus der du dich auf das Bett ziehst,
als wäre es ein sicheres Floß.
Zwar ist das noch keine Rettung,
aber alles weitere Fragen
wird vorerst entbehrlich.
Schon damit ist vieles gewonnen.

The Bed

The name of the disease carries you away
like a wave on the high seas.
The consequences won't be weighed for the time being.
Panic booms like water in both ears.

But there is a weariness
from which you pull yourself onto the bed
as if it were a lifeboat.
Admittedly it's not salvation,
but all other questions
become dispensable for the moment.
A lot has already been won.

Die Ameisen

Dieser Traum:
Zwischen Rinden
und mehlig gewordenem Stamm
rennen auf unbekannte Ziele gerichtet
in langer Paternoster-Kolonne
die Kerbtiere herunter, hinauf.
Siehst du dich nicht vor,
dann bist du der mehlig gewordene Stamm,
und deine Haut ist die Rinde.
Im Rückenmark wimmelt's,
dort ist es schwarz oder rot,
vor lauter Tieren.
Und wenn du aufwachst,
ist der Traum nicht zu Ende.
Dann krümmst du dich unter endlosen
Schmerzen,
suchst, in Schweiß gebadet,
den Schlaf, den du mit diesem Traum teuer
erkaufst.

The Ants

This dream:
Between bark
and mealy trunk
insects are racing up and down
in a long flaming column
their objectives unknown.
If you're not careful
you can become the mealy trunk
and your skin the bark.
Your spinal cord
swarms black or red,
full of living things.
And when you wake
the dream is not over.
Then you writhe in endless
pain,
bathed in sweat,
searching for the sleep bought so dearly
with this dream.

Die Stundung

Ein altes,
wuchertreibendes Weib
fordert so ihren Zins.
Gibst du dich der Täuschung hin,
sie habe dich diesmal vergessen,
dann steht sie
vor Deiner Tür,
kramt in alten Papieren,
wird bei jeder Stundung
rücksichtsloser und dreister.
Am Anfang
wies man ihr noch das Haus.
Jetzt weist sie's dir.
Alles ist so verschuldet
daß kaum noch Spielraum
für eigenes Planen bleibt.

Deferring Payment

An old,
tight-fisted bitch
demands the rent.
Don't trick yourself, thinking
that she'd forgotten you this time,
for there she stands
at your door,
rummaging in old papers,
more ruthless and bold
with each deferment.
At the beginning
she was turned away.
Now it's she who turns you away.
Everything is so in debt
that hardly any room is left
for your own planning.

Die Diagnose

Fast vierzig Jahre ist's her:
Nach der von den Müttern
verordneten Sonntag-Nachmittag-Andacht
ging ich mit Bruno, Georg und Norbert
zur Mergelgrube
zwischen Iller und Rot.
Dort holten wir werktags Fegsand
zum Säubern von Messer und Gabel
und im Herbst die nötige Menge
zum Aufbewahren der gelben Rüben.
Doch am Sonntag dachte keiner daran.
Am Sonntag wurde gewettet, wer die Steilwand
(es waren vielleicht sechs Meter)
am schnellsten schaffte.
Wünschte einer mit allen Mitteln
der erste zu sein,
reichten die Wurzelfasern
oder die wenigen Pflanzen sicher nicht aus,
den Eiligen festzuhalten.

Genauso ist's hier:
Erfährt ein Kranker die Diagnose
plötzlich und unvermittelt,
so schlägt er um sich
und fällt hinab in die Grube,
wird er mit Nachsicht behandelt,
dann hält er sich an der Wand,
rechnet sich Chancen aus,
und später sieht man
 – sofern man noch sieht –
dann vielleicht weiter.

The Diagnosis

Almost forty years gone by
since the days when our mothers
would order us to all-day Sunday church,
later I would go with Bruno, Georg and Norbert
to the sand pits
between the Iller and the Rot.
On weekdays we gathered polishing sand
for cleaning knives and forks
and in autumn as much as needed
for preserving yellow beets.
But nobody thought about that on Sunday.
Sundays we would bet on who could climb the steep wall
(about six meters tall)
the fastest.
If one of us wanted to be first
by any means,
like grabbing onto roots,
those few plants were certainly
not strong enough to hold the racer.

It's the same way here:
If a patient is suddenly
and abruptly diagnosed,
he struggles
and falls down into the pit,
while if he is treated with indulgence,
he will cling to the wall,
calculating his chances,
and only later will he see
– provided he still can see –
what's next.

Miquel Martí i Pol

Seit Jahren
lebt nun Miquel,
als Rentner entlassen,
mit seiner Frau und zwei Kindern
im kleinen Haus überm Ter,
nur einige Steinwürfe weit
von der durch ihn
bekannt gewordenen Fabrik.
Doch zum Steinewerfen
reichen die Kräfte nicht aus.
Er muß schon froh sein,
wenn er den Löffel zum Mund bringt.
Und sprechen kann er nicht mehr.
Aber über die Schreibmaschine
mahnt er die Freunde
jetzt, da der Henker tot ist,
das Morgen nicht zu verschlafen.

Hier in der Klinik
wirst du bestenfalls zum Kokon,
der eines Tages
 – wenn er nicht vorher erfriert –,
in dem für den Hubschrauber bezeichneten Platz
für die Dauer des Fluges
mit Lärm und Wirbel
der Klinik, doch nicht seiner Krankheit,
davon fliegt.

Miquel Martí i Pol

For years now
Miquel,
layed off, a pensioner,
has lived with his wife and two children
in the little house above the Ter
just a few stones' throw away
from the factory
made famous by him.
But he's not strong enough
to throw stones.
He must be grateful
if he can even get a spoon to his mouth.
And he can no longer speak.
But by typewriter
he warns his friends,
now that the hangman is dead,
not to oversleep tomorrow.

Here in the clinic
at best you'll be cocooned,
and one day
 – if you haven't already frozen up –
you'll take off from the helicopter pad
for the duration
of the noisy, whirling flight,
escaping the clinic,
but not your illness.

Die Gleichgültigkeit

Daß die Füße,
die Knie,
die Schenkel
allmählich gallertig werden
und spitz und stumpf,
warm und kalt
keine scharfen Konturen bezeichnen,
das ginge noch an.
Doch dieser Mehltau,
diese Gleichgültigkeit.
Selbst der endlich abgegangene Nagel
der kleinen Tochter
interessiert dich nur,
weil du es dir vornimmst.
Aber der Blick auf die Hand
wird ein mühsamer
und endloser Weg.
Und alles, was man dir sonst noch erzählt,
ist wie hinter Milchglas.

Indifference

That feet,
knees,
thighs
gradually become gelatinous
pin-pricky and dull,
warm and cold
no longer detecting sharp contours,
would still be bearable.
But this mildew,
this indifference.
Even the nail that finally came off
your little daughter's hand
you care about it only
because you put your mind to it.
But looking at her hand
will be tedious
and never-ending.
And everything else you are told
seems to exist behind frosted glass.

Heinz-Peter

Die Eltern meinten es gut:
Schenkten sie ihrem Buben
zur Belebung und Förderung
seiner Interessen ein kleines Labor,
dann schaffte der an Chemie Interessierte
sicher die Hürde des Numerus-Clausus.
Wenige Wochen später
fiel Heinz-Peter bewußtlos
aus seiner Tür.
Seitdem (bald sind es zwei Jahre)
lebt Heinz-Peter im Rollstuhl,
schreit zwar (vor allem bei Nacht),
aber sagt kein einziges Wort.
„Finden Sie nicht", fragt mich die Mutter,
„daß Heinz-Peter ein wenig aufmerkt,
wenn er Französisches hört?"
Bald darauf prüft sie, ob es nicht stimmt.
Im Rollstuhl sitzend
scheint Heinz-Peter zu lauschen,
wenn seine Mutter,
mit ihrem Finger nach oben zeigend,
ängstlich versichert:

„Tu vois, Heinz-Peter, le ciel est bleu."
Er hört es sich an,
mit blauen Augen,
unter blauer Mütze
und blauem Himmel
auf windgeschützter Terrasse.

Aber daß die Hoffnung der Mutter wohl trügte,
wer will ihr das sagen?

Heinz-Peter

The parents meant well:
To stimulate and foster his interests
they gave their boy,
a small chemistry set,
to improve his chances to
get into medical school.
A few weeks later
Heinz-Peter fell unconscious
out of his doorway.
Since then (soon it would be two years)
Heinz-Peter has lived in a wheelchair, screaming
(especially at night),
but doesn't say a word.
"Don't you think," his mother asks me,
"that Heinz-Peter pays some attention
when he hears French?"
Soon after, she checks to see if that's so.
Sitting in a wheelchair
Heinz-Peter seems to be listening
when his mother,
pointing her finger upwards
anxiously assures him:

"Tu vois, Heinz-Peter, le ciel est bleu."
He listens
with his blue eyes,
wearing a blue cap
under a blue sky
on a sheltered terrace.

But who will tell his mother
that her hope was likely an illusion?

Nacht

Manchmal schreit zwischen zehn Uhr
und elf aus seiner bewußtlosen Angst
im Gang gegenüber Heinz-Peter.
Dann kommt die Schwester,
und bis zum Morgen
hört man den Jungen nicht mehr.
Jetzt erst vernimmst du
im Halbschlaf
das Quaken der Frösche.
Wenn die Nacht klar ist
und gar noch der Mond scheint,
hören sie selten vor drei Uhr schon auf.
Bald ahnt man den Tag.
Um halb vier Uhr ruft in den Wäldern
der Kuckuck, und kaum eine Stunde später
kommen Spatzen und andere Vögel.
Nach fünf Uhr
ist die lange Nacht
der Schwestern zu Ende.
Dann gehen sie schlafen,
während hier wie immer
der Alltag beginnt.

Night

Sometimes between ten and eleven
Heinz-Peter screams from instinctive fear
in the corridor across the way.
Then the nurse comes
and you don't hear the boy again
until morning.
And then, half asleep,
you hear
the croaking of frogs.
When the night is clear
and even more when the moon is shining
they seldom stop before three AM.
Soon you can sense daybreak.
At half-past three a cuckoo calls in the woods, and
barely an hour later
sparrows and other birds come along.
After five
the nurses' long night shift
is done.
Then they go to sleep,
while here everyday life
begins as usual.

Andreas

Man war es sich und dem Jungen
nach glücklich bestandenem Abitur
beinahe schuldig:
ein rasantes Auto.
Nach der Party geschah es:
Der Baum war gerammt,
der Wagen zertrümmert,
und Andreas bleib lange Zeit
in der Klinik.
Als er herauskam,
lachte er viel –
zuviel für sein Alter,
und was er sagte,
war nicht auf Maturaniveau.
Der Rückwärtsgang in die Kindheit
bleibt eingerastet,
kuppeln und schalten
verschlägt nichts,
der Kopf bleibt verformt.

Aber rasante Fahrten im Rollstuhl
erlauben Andreas manchmal
Augenblicke des Spiels
oder vielleicht des Vergessens.

Andreas

They almost owed it
to themselves, as well as to him
for graduating high school:
a speedy car.
It happened after the party:
The tree was rammed
the car was smashed,
and Andreas stayed in the hospital
a long time.
When he came out
he laughed a lot,
too much for his age,
and what he said
was not at graduate-level.
The reverse gear to childhood
had snapped into place,
and trying to shift back
doesn't work,
his head stays deformed.

But speedy rides in his wheelchair
sometimes allow Andreas
moments of play
or maybe of forgetting.

Der Aufzug

Im Schwimmbad
sind sie beinahe munter.
Doch dann kommt der Aufzug,
und sie plumpen in die übliche
Schwerkraft zurück.
Bänder gürten und halten fest.
Der Rollstuhl wartet.
Die Illusion geht zu Ende.
Kaulquappen gleich,
mit weit geöffneten Augen,
kommen sie aus dem Wasser,
werden von Pflegern getrocknet
und wieder ins Zimmer gebracht.

The Lift

In the pool
they are almost cheerful.
But then the lift comes
and plops them back into their normal
gravitational field.
Tied and held with belts.
The wheelchair is waiting.
The illusion ends.
Like tadpoles,
with wide-open eyes,
they come out of the water,
are dried by their attendants
and brought back into their rooms.

Der Tümpel

Vor meinem Zimmer
sieht man das Wasser schimmern.
Aber geht man
den mit Steinplatten
und weißgestrichnem Geländer
bis zum Weiher markierten Weg,
dann liegt das Wasser
deutlich vor Augen
und die baumbestandene Insel
mitten im Teich.
Überall Tannen, Birken und Weiden,
und im Norden
das Ufer mit Schilf.
Dort stehen manchmal
die weißen Enten
und watscheln
– wer gibt das Kommando? –
behäbig ins Wasser hinab.

The Pond

Outside my room
you can see the water shimmer.
But when you go
up to the pond
along the path with the stone slabs
and white-painted railing,
then the water lies
directly in front of you,
with a tree-lined island
in the middle of the pond.
Fir, birch and willow everywhere,
and to the north
a reedy shore.
Sometimes there are white ducks
standing there
that waddle slowly
 – who gives the order? –
down into the water.

Die Evers-Diät

Wer auf die Madonna in Lourdes schwört,
braucht keine anderen Pilgerfahrten.

Vor dem Draht an der Weide,
über fliegengeschwärzten Fladen,
erklärte runden und sonnengebräunten Gesichts
eine irritierend gesunde Passantin,
wäre sie, wie so viele hier,
an Multipler Sklerose erkrankt,
wäre sie sicher nicht da.
Sie habe im Fernsehen noch gar nicht lange
mit diesen Augen gesehen,
daß Doktor Evers in seiner Klinik
die Rollstuhlpatienten fast ausnahmslos heile,
hier sei es nicht so.
Drum wäre ihr keinerlei Weg zu weit
und wären keinerlei Kosten zuviel.
Das sei ihre Meinung.
Dann schob sie den Draht zur Seite
und stapfte, für jede Zukunft gerüstet,
zwischen fliegengeschwärzten Fladen
schräg über die Wiesen davon.

The Evers Diet

She who swears by the Madonna of Lourdes
doesn't need any other pilgrimage.

In front of the pasture gate,
among cowflops blackened by flies,
an irritatingly healthy passer-by
with a chubby, tanned face
explained – that if she were suffering from multiple
sclerosis
like so many here –
she certainly wouldn't be among them.
She had seen on TV not too long ago
with her own eyes
that in *his* clinic Doctor Evers
can heal wheelchair patients almost
without exception,
but not here.
No road would be too long for her
and no cost would be too high.
That was her opinion.
Then she pushed the wire aside
and trudged across the meadow among cowflops
blackened by flies,
all geared up for anything.

Im oberen Rottal

Im oberen Rottal
hat die Bachregulierung
die Bukolik begradigt.
Der Bauer nahm es in Kauf,
verglich er die Wiesen
früher und jetzt.
Und nicht zu glauben:
Fischreiher flogen noch nie
in solchen Mengen
vom Ufer auf.
Ging ich als kleiner Junge
an heißen Tagen zum Baden,
kamen die Großen,
hoben mich über den Kopf
und warfen mich schreiend
und hilflos zappelnd
ins tiefe Wasser der Gumpe
und lachten sich
schier zu Tode,
wenn ich, prustend
und um mich schlagend,
vom großen Bruder
geholt und beruhigt wurde.
Heute badet
keiner mehr dort
und versucht es jemand,
hat er am anderen Tag
einen Ausschlag.

In the Upper Rot Valley

In the upper Rot valley
stream regulation
corrected unspoiled nature.
Farmers accepted it
after comparing the meadows
then and now.
And believe it or not:
never once
had so many herons
flown from the banks.
As a little boy I went
swimming on hot days,
and the bigger boys
lifted me over their heads
and threw me screaming
and helplessly struggling
into the deepest water
and laughed themselves
almost to death
when I, sputtering
and flailing around,
was rescued and calmed down
by my big brother.
Today, nobody swims
there anymore
and if someone tries to,
in a few days
he'll break out in a rash.

Mit Blütenzweigen im Arm

Die junge Patientin
aus Ehingen an der Donau
landete mit ihrem Wagen
in einem für Waren bestimmten Fenster
nicht weit vom Marktplatz.
Es war nicht Exhibitionismus,
sondern ein Kreislaufkollaps.
Zum Glück war nichts Ernstes passiert.
Doch seit dem vierundzwanzigsten Vierten
kann sie nicht mehr gehen.
Schon lange beschäftigt die Ärzte
das diagnostische Rätsel.
Bisher ohne Erfolg.
Auch der Computer
wurde nicht schlauer.
Hier verschaffte man ihr
schnell einen Rollstuhl.
Eine nicht ernstlich
behinderte Kranke
fährt sie mitunter hinaus.
Dort sah ich sie eben
mit Blütenzweigen im Arm
lächelnd und plaudernd,
und alles sah aus,
als sei die Szene
nur fürs Theater gestellt.

With Flowering Branches in her Arms

The young patient
from Ehingen on the Danube
landed with her car
in a shop window
not far from the market place.
It wasn't showing off,
but circulatory collapse.
Fortunately, there was no serious damage.
But since the twenty-fourth of April
she can't walk anymore.
Doctors have been busy for a long time
trying to solve the diagnostic puzzle,
so far unsuccessfully.
The computer
was no smarter.
Here, she was quickly put
into a wheelchair.
A lightly disabled patient,
sometimes
wheels her outside.
I just saw her out there
with branches of flowers in her arms
smiling and chatting,
and everything looked
as if the scene
were made just for the stage.

Die Telefonistin

Je nach Temperament
reagieren die Kranken,
wenn die querschnittgelähmte
Rollstuhlpatientin
den Sonntagabend
telefonierend verbringt.
Choleriker
rollen das Weiße im Auge.
Melancholiker
schleichen sich ratlos davon,
Patienten mit Energie
rücken näher und näher
an ihre Lehne heran.
Doch das stört sie kaum:
„Mutti, ich habe eben
ein Markstück hineingeworfen,
erzähl mir noch etwas
....
Ich habe noch
siebzig Pfennig im Automaten,
die laß' ich doch nicht verfallen.
Schau bitte nach,
ob das rote Buch
im rechten Regal steht...
....
findest du nicht?

Ist doch nicht möglich!
Schau doch noch einmal nach!
....
Siehst du, ich hab es gesagt,
aber nun erzähl mir doch etwas,
inzwischen hab ich den Speicher
schon wieder gefüllt.
Ich hab noch
achtzig Pfennig im Automaten.
Also Mutti,
die laß ich doch nicht verfallen
...."

Someone on the Phone

Sick people react
according to their characters,
when the paraplegic
wheelchair patient
spends Sunday evening
making calls.
The irascible types
roll their eyes,
melancholics
slink away at a loss for what to do,
and energetic patients
move closer and closer
to her armrest.
But that hardly bothers her:
"Mom, I've just
put a whole mark into the phone,
so tell me something more.

....
I still have
seventy pfennigs worth of time
I don't want to lose.
Please check
whether the red book
is on the right-hand shelf ...

....
It's not there?

That's impossible!
Check it out again!
....
You see, I said it was there,
but now tell me something more
since I have filled up
the phone again.
I still have
eighty pfennigs deposited.
So Mom,
I'm not going to let them go to waste
...."

Die Hand

Die neue Kranke
im Zimmer links
heult auf oder stöhnt.
Die Besucher gehen
mit verstörten Gesichtern
davon.
Doch schlimmer ist ihre Hand,
die wandauf, wandab
raschelt und kratzt.
Was will sie,
was hat sie vor?
Täglich wird
die Trennmauer dünner.
Wer garantiert mir,
daß ihre Finger
nicht plötzlich bei Nacht
mit mir im Raum sind
und auf meiner Haut
suchen und kratzen?

Hand

The new patient
in the room on the left
howls or groans.
Visitors
leave there
looking distraught.
But her hand is worse,
swishing and scratching
up the wall, down the wall.
What does she want,
what is she up to?
Everyday
the dividing wall becomes thinner.
Who will promise me
that suddenly at night
her fingers
will not be in the room with me
searching for, scratching
at my skin?

Die Coppelius-Puppe

Die Patientin scheint aus E.T.A. Hoffmann entsprungen.
Coppelius war der Meister ihrer Mechanik.
Urplötzlich rennt sie los,
läßt ihre Gefährten bald weit zurück.
Doch wenn ein winziges Hindernis kommt,
verliert sie das Gleichgewicht,
knickt in die Knie,
fällt hin.
Dieses Mal ging es noch gut.
Passanten sahen sie stürzen,
rannten schnell zu ihr hin,
stellten sie wieder auf ihre Füße,
und schon lief sie wieder.
Die Feder
war nirgends gebrochen.

The Coppelius Doll

The patient seems to be right out of E.T.A. Hoffmann
as if Coppelius had made her clockworks.
All of a sudden she runs off
leaving her companions far behind.
But when a tiny obstacle comes up
she loses her balance,
her knees give way
and she falls.
This time nothing happened.
Passers-by saw her fall,
ran to her quickly,
put her back on her feet,
and she was running again.
No springs
were broken.

Die Pony-Ranch

Nicht weit vom Eingang,
wo seit mehreren Tagen
hinter dem Wohnheim für Pfleger
und sonstigem Personal
nun lila die Rhododendren blühn,
verweist eine hölzerne Tafel
auf den Weg zur Pony-Ranch.
An Wochenenden
dürfen Kinder
für 50 Pfennig
auf Pferderücken
am Zügel geführt
jeweils fünf Runden drehn.
Aber an Wochentagen
sind eher Patienten die Gäste.
Gestützt auf befreundete Arme,
am Geländer sich haltend,
mit Stöcken gerüstet
oder auf Rollstuhlrädern
hastig hinuntergeschoben,
machen sie sich auf den Weg,
als seien sie nun
endgültig frei.

In der Ranch gibt es Kaffee
und einen Ausschank mit Bier,
von den über offenem Feuer
brutzelnden Würsten
unter Tabak und Zigarren
gar nicht zu reden.
Wer bis hierher den Weg schafft,
ist – mit Maßen –
sein eigener Herr.
Zugegeben:
Der Rückweg bergauf
ist etwas beschwerlich.
Aber die Stimmung
von Aufbruch und Ausbruch hält an.
Etwas von der Freiheit der Ponys
vermittelt die Ranch ihren Gästen,
auch denen mit Rollstuhl
und denen am Arm ihrer Freunde.

The Pony Ranch

Not far from the entrance,
behind the nurses' and
staff housing,
where for several days,
purple rhododendrons bloom,
a wooden plaque
points the way to the Pony Ranch.
Weekends,
for 50 pfennigs,
children can sit
on horseback
led by the reins
for five laps at a time.
But on weekdays
the patients tend to be the guests.
Leaning on friendly arms,
holding on to the railing,
armed with canes
or on wheelchairs
pushed briskly down there,
they make their way
as if they were now
finally free.

There's coffee at the Ranch
and a bar with beer,
not to mention the sausages
sizzling over an open fire
and underneath,
tobacco and cigars.
Whoever manages to get here
is – within limits –
his own master.
Granted:
the way back uphill
is a bit difficult.
But the mood
of new possibilities and breakout persists.
The Ranch provides its guests with
something of the freedom of the ponies,
even for those in wheelchairs
or on the arms of their friends.

Die Wanderung

Der Spaziergang
tief in den Wald
bis zur Höhe
zwischen Rottum and Rottal.
In der Ferne der schon wieder
klare und sonnige Horizont.
Am liebsten ist mir die Bank
unter dem Jägersitz.
Hinter den Leitersprossen
sieht man die bräunlichen Ähren
des Roggenfelds.
Darüber ziehen die Lerchen
ihre Spiralen.
Und immer wieder
fliegt aus den Bäumen
ein nur selten sichtbarer Vogel auf.
Mit der Klinik hat das nichts mehr zu tun.
Kaum ein Kranker wagt sich dorthin.
Wer dort ist,
vergißt Katheder und Tomographie.

Hike

The walk
deep in the forest
up to the heights
between the Rottum and Rot Valley.
In the distance again,
the clear and sunny horizon.
My favorite is the bench
under the hunter's seat.
Behind the rungs of the ladder
you can see the brownish growth
of the rye fields.
The larks
spiral over them.
And again and again
a fleeting bird
flies from the trees.
All this has no relation to the clinic.
Hardly any patient dares go there.
Whoever is there
forgets catheters and x-rays.

Das Geländer

Das weiße Geländer hier oben,
das weiße Geländer dort unten:
dazwischen die Straße,
die keinerlei Stütze bietet.
So bin ich sicher
vom Tisch oder Stuhl zur Mutter gerannt
und wurde gefeiert,
wenn es gelang.
Hier sind's dreißig Schritte,
mit dem nie überschaubaren Stück
der autobefahrenen Straße.
Nach wenigen Tagen
wurde der erste
Versuch unternommen,
und nach einigen Wochen
spazierte ich täglich
mit auf dem Rücken gefalteten Händen
bis in die Wälder hinein.

The Railing

The white railing up here,
the white railing down there:
and between them the road
offering no support.
Like the way I must have run
from the table or chair to my mother
and was applauded,
when I made it.
Here it's thirty steps
including the never-friendly stretch
of the busy road.
After a few days
I made my
first attempt,
and after a few weeks
I strolled into the woods
every day
with my hands folded behind my back.

Die Birke

Die ersten Tage waren die schlimmsten.
Lesen verbot mir die doppelte Sicht,
Schreiben die unsichere Hand.
Und Denken war ein mahlender Bagger.
Doch fast immer wehte Nord-Ost.
Ich erinnerte mich an den Sund
und das in frischer Brise
sich drehende Artefakt von Alexander Calder.
Hier mußte ich mich bescheiden
mit Birkenästen und
um sich schlagenden Zweigen.
Ein Mobile war auch dies.
Vielleicht entwarf es im wirren Tohuwabohu
erste Akzente,
Strophen und wohltuenden Rhythmus.
Und so war der Tag,
die Dämmerung morgens und abends
durch Blätter und Birkenäste
deutlich markiert.

The Birch Tree

The first days were the worst.
Seeing double, I couldn't read,
my hand trembled too much to write,
and thinking was like a grinding backhoe.
But the Northeast wind was constant.
I remembered the sound
and that Alexander Calder mobile
that turned in the breeze.
Here I had to make do
with birch branches and
the clatter of twigs.
These were also a mobile.
Maybe they suggested the first pulse
in some chaotic hubbub
with its stanzas and soothing rhythm.
Just so was my day,
the half-light of dawn and evening
marked clearly
through leaves and birch branches.

Stuten und Töchter

„Wenn ich an andere Frauen
in meinem Alter denke,
dann kann ich mich
über meinen Mann
und seine Eltern
in keiner Weise beklagen.
Er blieb bei mir,
auch als ich im Rollstuhl lebte,
und seine Mutter
nahm beide Kinder zu sich.

So hielt ich die schlimmsten
Wochen und Monate aus.
Aber mein Vater
verdrängt die Multiple Sklerose der Tochter.
Das kann doch nicht wahr sein.
Erkrankt ihm ein Pferd
in seinem Gestüte,
dann wacht er bei ihm auch
mehrere Nächte.
Doch seitdem ich hier bin,
– das sind jetzt drei Wochen –
hat er kein einziges Mal
nach mir geschaut."

Horses and Daughters

"When I think about
other women my age
I can in no way
complain about
my husband
and his parents.
He stayed with me
even when I was in a wheelchair,
and his mother
took in both children to care for.

That's how I got through
the worst weeks and months.
But my father
ignores his daughter's multiple sclerosis.
How can this be?
If one of the horses
in his stable gets sick
he stays up with it
even for several nights.
But since I've been here,
 – three weeks now –
he has not once
come to see me."

Der alte Mann

Der alte Mann,
dessen Fahrrad an einem Baum lehnt,
saß im Schatten der großen Buche.
Ich lobte
die vielen Bänke im Walde,
die gute Luft
und die Täler.
Er lud mich zum Sitzen,
sprach dieses und jenes
und kannte noch meinen Vater.
„Und ob ich ihn kannte!
Bei den Innungsversammlungen
in Ochsenhausen
hörte man gerne auf ihn.
Einmal,
ich erinnere mich daran genau,
blähte der Obermeister
sich wie ein Gockel,
die Schuster vom Land,
das seien elende Pfuscher.

Ihr Vater meldete sich
und erzählte:
‚Kam vor einigen Tagen
ein Kunde und brachte
rahmengenähte, mit Taxen besohlte Schuhe,
– Nun sagen Sie mal,
wer machte die Pfuschreperatur?
– Der Obermeister persönlich.
Soll ich kommentieren?‘
Da schmunzelten alle,
nur der Verspottete nicht.
Wann ist ihr Vater gestorben?"
Am 3. September
neunzehnhundertundvierzig.

The Old Man

The old man,
whose bike is leaning against a tree,
sat in the shade of a large beech.
I praised
the many benches in the forest
the clean air
and the valleys.
He invited me to sit down,
talked about this and that
and said he knew my father.
"Did I know him!
At the guild meetings
in Ochsenhausen
people loved to listen to him.
Once,
I remember exactly,
the master shoemaker crowed
like a rooster
that cobblers from the countryside,
are miserable bunglers.

Your father spoke up
and told this story:
'A few days ago
a customer came in
with some hand-sewn shoes re-soled with
tacks.
 – Now tell us
who did such a botched repair?
 – The master personally.'
Need I say more?'
Everyone chuckled except
the ridiculed master.
When did your father die?"
September 3rd
Nineteen forty.

Women's Lib

Daß sie keinen BH trägt,
erinnert vielleicht an die 68er Jahre
oder an die Protestbewegung
von Women's Lib.
Aber für ihre Tage im Rollstuhl
bringt es nicht viel.
Dort rechnet sie nach,
ob das ganze Unglück
politisch und agitatorisch zu nutzen ist.
Das hülfe vielleicht über
die Schwierigkeiten hinweg.
Aber hier findet Protest keine Ohren.
Hier schreist du vor Schmerz und fällst,
schon lange bevor die Stimme verstummt,
in eigensinniges Schweigen.

Women's Lib

That she's not wearing a bra
may remind you of '68
or of Women's Lib
protests.
But it doesn't figure much
into her days in a wheelchair.
Now she's thinking about
whether the whole accident
might be used politically or as agit-prop.
Perhaps that might help her
over her difficulties.
But protest finds no ears here.
Here you scream in pain and fall
well before your voice fades
into obstinate silence.

Pfingsten

Tagelang
sah ich den Kranken,
der blakenden Blicks
in seinem Zimmer
und manchmal im Gang
sich von Schwestern und Wärtern
verpflegen ließ.
Meinen Gruß ließ er unerwidert.
Aber heute sitzt er auf der Terrasse.
Eine junge Patientin hat ihre Beine
– die Knöchel sind kaum zu sehen:
so voller Wasser sind die Gelenke –
auf einen Tisch gelegt.
Als wäre Pfingsten
löst sich die Zunge
des stummen Zimmernachbars
und die Verkrampfung seiner Gebärden.
Doch seine Avancen werden übel belohnt:
„Glotz nicht so geil,
behalt dein Gerede für dich,
bei dir ist doch nichts mehr los,
drum stör mich nicht
bei meinem Flirt
mit dem netten Jungen
hier neben mir."

„Bringen Sie mich zum WC!",
wandte der Mann sich an mich.
„Lassen Sie ihn,
er ist doch nur faul,
läßt sich im Rollstuhl verwöhnen",
sagte die Rollstuhlpatientin
mit den geschwollenen Knöcheln,
als ich ihn schnell durch die Tür schob.

Pentecost

For days
I saw the sick guy with
the firey glance
in his room
and sometimes in the corridor
allowing himself to be cared for by
nurses and orderlies.
He never responded to my greeting.
But today he's sitting on the terrace.
A young woman patient has her legs
stretched out on a table.
 – her joints so full of fluid her ankles are barely
visible.
My mute hallmate's
tongue
and his cramped gestures,
loosen as if it were Pentecost.
But his advances are badly rewarded:
"Don't look so horny,
and keep your mouth to yourself.
You can't get it up anymore,
so don't disturb
my flirting
with the nice young man
here next to me."
The man turned to me

"Take me to the toilet!"
"Don't listen to him.
He's just lazy,
wants to be pampered in a wheelchair,"
said the wheelchair patient
with the swollen ankles,
as I quickly pushed him through the door.

Tat twam asi

Die Dauerpatienten,
die Pflegefälle kenne ich kaum.
Haben sie etwas zu sagen,
tun sie's mit kreischender Stimme,
grüße ich sie,
stört sie's
in der Monotonie ihres Tags.
Vielleicht bin auch ich
daran schuldig.
Aber wer will diese Zukunft
schon überstürzen?
Solange Post kommt,
das Telefon sich meldet
und Besucher mit mir
bis tief in die Wälder wandern.

Tat twam asi

I hardly know the long-term patients,
the nursing care cases.
When they have something to say,
they say it in a screeching voice,
and if I greet them
it disturbs
the monotony of their days.
Maybe I'll become
that way too.
But who wants to rush
such a future?
As long as the mail comes,
the phone keeps ringing,
and visitors hike
deep into the woods with me.

Die Heimkehr

„Als der Arzt
mir heute sagte,
ich könne morgen nach Hause,
brach ich in Tränen aus.
Da gab er noch einige Tage hinzu."
Das erzählte mir eben
die freundliche Frau mit der Thrombose
am linken Bein.
„Wie soll ich
das Drunter und Drüber,
das ich daheim vorfinden werde,
in meinem Zustand
in Ordnung bringen?
Beim bloßen Gedanken
brach ich in Panik aus.
Aber wenn ich jetzt daran denke,
daß ich noch eineinhalb Stunden
bis zum Abendessen
mich langweilen muß...?"
„Mit Rosenkranzbeten
käm es auf einen Versuch an.
Man braucht ja nicht gleich zu erwarten,
jemand nehme im Himmel droben den Hörer ab.
Einfach mal so."
Sie lächelt,
entschuldigt sich dann:
„Mein Bein braucht wieder Bewegung.
Doch morgen sehn wir uns wieder."

Going Home

"When the doctor
told me today
that I could go home tomorrow,
I burst into tears.
So he gave me a few more days."
That was what the friendly woman with thrombosis
in her left leg
was just telling me.
"In my condition,
how will I
deal with the
holy mess
I'll find at my place?
I panic
just thinking about it.
But when I think now
that I have to get through
an hour and a half
until dinner...?"
"How about saying the rosary?
It's worth a try.
Just don't expect
someone in heaven to pick up the phone right away
just like that."
She smiles,
then apologizes:
"I have to move my leg now.
But we'll see each other again tomorrow."

Johannes Hösle was born in 1929 in Erolzheim, a town in the district of Biberach in Baden-Württemberg, Germany. Between 1961 and 1965, he was the director of the Goethe-Institute in Milan, Italy. From 1968-1995, he was Professor of Romance Languages at the University of Regensburg. This collection of poetry was written in 1977 during a stay at the Dietenbronn Neurological Clinic. He died in 2017 in Regensburg.

Marc Estrin, translator, is a novelist and musician living in Burlington, Vermont.

Gisela Conrad (1944-2019), graphic artist, lived and worked in Regensburg. The cover image is *Langsam auf dem Weg*, a print from her series, *Terra Incognita*.

About Fomite

A fomite is a medium capable of transmitting infectious organisms from one individual to another.

"The activity of art is based on the capacity of people to be infected by the feelings of others." Tolstoy, *What Is Art?*

Writing a review on Amazon, Good Reads, Shelfari, Library Thing or other social media sites for readers will help the progress of independent publishing. To submit a review, go to the book page on any of the sites and follow the links for reviews. Books from independent presses rely on reader-to-reader communications.

For more information or to order any of our books, visit:
http://www.fomitepress.com/our-books.html

More poetry from Fomite...

Anna Blackmer — Hexagrams
L. Brown — Loopholes
Sue D. Burton — Little Steel
David Cavanagh— Cycling in Plato's Cave
James Connolly — Picking Up the Bodies
Greg Delanty — Loosestrife
Mason Drukman — Drawing on Life
J. C. Ellefson — Foreign Tales of Exemplum and Woe
Tina Escaja/Mark Eisner — Caida Libre/Free Fall
Anna Faktorovich — Improvisational Arguments
Barry Goldensohn — Snake in the Spine, Wolf n the Heart
Barry Goldensohn — The Hundred Yard Dash Man
Barry Goldensohn — The Listener Aspires to the Condition of Music
R. L. Green — When You Remember Deir Yassin
Gail Holst-Warhaft — Lucky Country
Raymond Luczak — A Babble of Objects
Kate Magill — Roadworthy Creature, Roadworthy Craft
Tony Magistrale — Entanglements
Gary Mesick — General Discharge
Andreas Nolte — Mascha: The Poems of Mascha Kaléko
Sherry Olson — Four-Way Stop
Brett Ortler — Lessons of the Dead

David Polk — Drinking the River
Janice Miller Potter — Meanwell
Janice Miller Potter — Thoreau's Umbrella
Philip Ramp — The Melancholy of a Life as the Joy of Living It
          Slowly Chills
Joseph D. Reich — A Case Study of Werewolves
Joseph D. Reich — Connecting the Dots to Shangrila
Joseph D. Reich — The Derivation of Cowboys and Indians
Joseph D. Reich — The Hole That Runs Through Utopia
Joseph D. Reich — The Housing Market
Kenneth Rosen and Richard Wilson — Gomorrah
Fred Rosenblum — Playing Chicken with an Iron Horse
Fred Rosenblum — Vietnumb \
David Schein — My Murder and Other Local News
Lawrence Schimel — Desert Memory: Poems of Jeannette L. Clariond
Harold Schweizer — Miriam's Book
Scott T. Starbuck — Carbonfish Blues
Scott T. Starbuck — Hawk on Wire
Scott T. Starbuck — Industrial Oz
Seth Steinzor — Among the Lost
Seth Steinzor — To Join the Lost
Susan Thomas — In the Sadness Museum
Susan Thomas — The Empty Notebook Interrogates Itself
Sharon Webster — Everyone Lives Here
Tony Whedon — The Tres Riches Heures
Tony Whedon — The Falkland Quartet
Claire Zoghb — Dispatches from Everest

Dual Language
Vito Bonito/Alison Grimaldi Donahue — Soffiata Via/Blown Away
Antonello Borra/Blossom Kirschenbaum — Alfabestiario
Antonello Borra/Blossom Kirschenbaum — AlphaBetaBestiaro
Antonello Borra/Anis Memon — Fabbrica delle idee/
          The Factory of Ideas
Aristea Papalexandrou/Philip Ramp — Μας προσπερνά/It's Overtaking Us
Mikis Theodoraksi/Gail Holst-Warhaft — The House with the Scorpions
Paolo Valesio/Todd Portnowitz — La Mezzanotte di Spoleto/
          Midnight in Spoleto

www.ingramcontent.com/pod-product-compliance
Lightning Source LLC
Chambersburg PA
CBHW031247120626
46545CB00007B/2689